W9-BAQ-551

IF YOU WERE A KID DURING THE
Civil War

BY WIL MARA • ILLUSTRATED BY ROGER ZANNI

CHILDREN'S PRESS ®

An Imprint of Scholastic Inc.

Content Consultant
James Marten, PhD, Professor and Chair, History Department, Marquette University

Photo credits ©: 9: Everett Collection; 11: Library of Congress; 13: Roger-Viollet/The Image Works; 15: National Archives and Records Administration; 17: Library of Congress; 19: Old Paper Studios/Alamy Images; 21: JT Vintage/age fotostock; 23: Buyenlarge/Getty Images; 25: Atomazul/Shutterstock, Inc.; 27: Niday Picture Library/Alamy Images.

Library of Congress Cataloging-in-Publication Data
Names: Mara, Wil, author. | Zanni, Roger, illustrator.
Title: If you were a kid during the Civil War / by Wil Mara ; illustrated by
   Roger Zanni.
Description: New York, NY : Children's Press, 2016. | Series: If you were a
   kid | Includes bibliographical references and index.
Identifiers: LCCN 2016008153| ISBN 9780531219690 (library binding) |
   ISBN 9780531221662 (pbk.)
Subjects: LCSH: United States—History—Civil War, 1861–1865—Participation,
   Juvenile—Juvenile literature. | United States—History—Civil War,
   1861–1865—Children—Juvenile literature. | Children—United
   States—History—19th century—Juvenile literature.
Classification: LCC E540.C47 M37 2016 | DDC 973.7083—dc23
LC record available at http://lccn.loc.gov/2016008153

Scholastic Inc., 557 Broadway, New York, NY 10012.

TABLE OF CONTENTS

A Different Way of Life

In 1861, war broke out in the United States of America. This time, the U.S. military was not fighting against another country. Southern states—called the Confederacy—were fighting against Northern states—called the Union. Imagine you were a kid during the Civil War. The country was at risk of permanently splitting in two. Your own friends, relatives, and neighbors might have fought on opposite sides of the war. Also, everyday life was much different than it is today. Many people grew their own food, and stores had limited supplies. Medical care was not as advanced as it is today. This made fighting even more dangerous.

Turn the page to find out what it was like to live in a country divided in two. You will see that life today is a lot different than it was in the past.

Meet Sarah!

This is Sarah Pierce. She's a spirited girl who lives on a farm in Virginia. Her family grows most of their own food. They chop their own wood to make fires for cooking and heating. Sarah's father makes money building and fixing things for people in town. Her mother keeps the house clean and cooks the meals. Sarah often helps out with these chores. When she has free time, she loves to walk along the wooded paths near her home . . .

Meet James!

James Hood is Sarah's best friend. His family lives just a couple of miles from Sarah's. They have a small farm, and James often helps out.

James's parents used to be friendly with the Pierces. But since the war started, they haven't been speaking to each other. The Hoods support the Confederates, while the Pierces believe in the Union. James and Sarah are worried that their parents will never be friends again . . .

It was a beautiful spring afternoon in 1864. James was hurrying to meet Sarah. Almost every day, the two friends met halfway between their homes to visit. When James got to the usual spot, Sarah was already waiting. They shared a snack and talked about how their families didn't get along anymore.

"Don't worry, though," said Sarah. "My parents still like you!"

"That's a relief!" James answered with a smile.

A SMALL WORLD

Today, it is easy to travel. You can ride your bike to the other side of your town. You can ride in a car to the other side of your state. You can even take an airplane to the other side of the world! People didn't have these choices in the mid-1800s. They usually walked or rode horses to travel. To go longer distances, they relied on trains.

A Secret Service agent rides a horse during the Civil War's Battle of Antietam in 1862.

James woke early the next morning. As he opened the door to go outside, he heard yelling and gunfire in the distance. He could also smell smoke. It was a battle, and it was happening very close to his home.

James was worried about Sarah and her family. He wanted to make sure they were okay. But his parents wouldn't let him leave. They told him to stay inside until it was safe.

A COUNTRY SPLIT IN TWO

The main reason for the Civil War was the disagreement over **slavery**. In the South, many farmers relied on slaves to work on their farms and in their houses without pay. But other people knew slavery was cruel. Northern leaders such as President Abraham Lincoln wanted to make it illegal. Starting in December 1860, the Southern states began **seceding** from the rest of the country to avoid giving up slavery.

An enslaved family in South Carolina during the Civil War

The fighting didn't stop until that night. The next morning, James's parents finally allowed him to check on Sarah. She was already waiting for him on the trail. She explained that the battle had been frightening, but she and her family were okay. Confederate soldiers had stomped through their crops and broken a window on their shed, though.

James suggested they go to a high ridge and look down at the battlefield. Sarah was curious to see it, too.

A BATTLE IN YOUR BACKYARD

During the Civil War, you might find soldiers fighting in your yard. This was true whether you lived in the South or even some parts of the North. Many battles took place in areas where people lived. Even those who didn't want to fight were at risk of being hurt or having their homes destroyed.

Ruined buildings in Richmond, Virginia, at the end of the Civil War

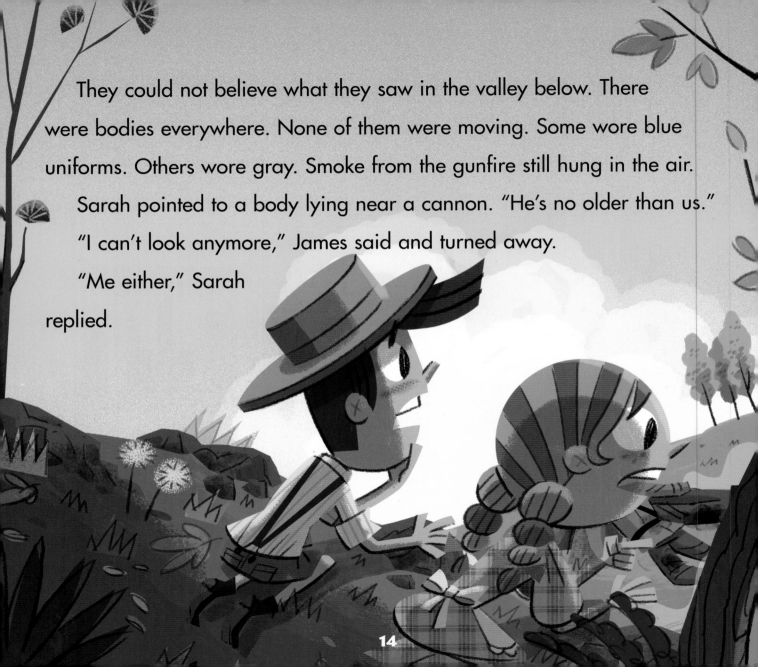

They could not believe what they saw in the valley below. There were bodies everywhere. None of them were moving. Some wore blue uniforms. Others wore gray. Smoke from the gunfire still hung in the air. Sarah pointed to a body lying near a cannon. "He's no older than us."

"I can't look anymore," James said and turned away.

"Me either," Sarah replied.

CHILD SOLDIERS

Today, you cannot usually join the military until you are at least 18 years old. This was also the normal **enlistment** age during the Civil War. However, that rule was often ignored. Children as young as 11 joined many battles. Some historians believe as many as one out of every five soldiers may have been under 18.

Some young soldiers played drums as troops marched into battle.

15

Suddenly, the two friends heard someone yelling. "That sounds like someone calling for help!" Sarah said. They followed the sound to a wooded hillside. There they saw a man lying facedown on the ground. There was blood all over his blue uniform. James and Sarah ran toward him. As they neared, he looked up. James gasped. The soldier was black.

FIGHTING FOR FREEDOM

During the Civil War, many black men joined the Union army to help defeat the Confederates. Their numbers grew larger as the Union won battles and set people free from slavery. Many of these newly free men decided to join the fight. By the end of the war, around one out of ten Union soldiers was black.

A black Union soldier poses for a portrait in his uniform.

The soldier's breathing was heavy. When Sarah tried to look at his wounds, he let out a scream of pain.

"He's been shot," she said. "And he has a fever. Come help me, James. We'll bring him back to my mother so she can patch him up." She turned and saw James shaking his head.

"No," he said. "My dad told me not to trust black people."

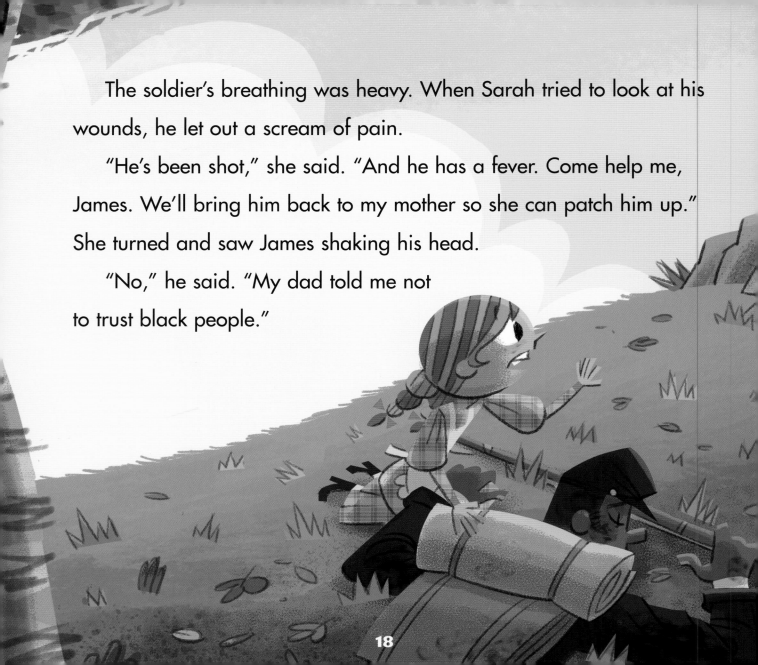

NOT TREATED EQUALLY

During the Civil War, **racism** was a major problem even in the North. Black people had almost no legal rights. They were not allowed to go to school or get good jobs. If you were white, you wouldn't have had any black classmates. If you were black, you might not have been able to go to school.

An all-white class gathers for a photo not long after the Civil War.

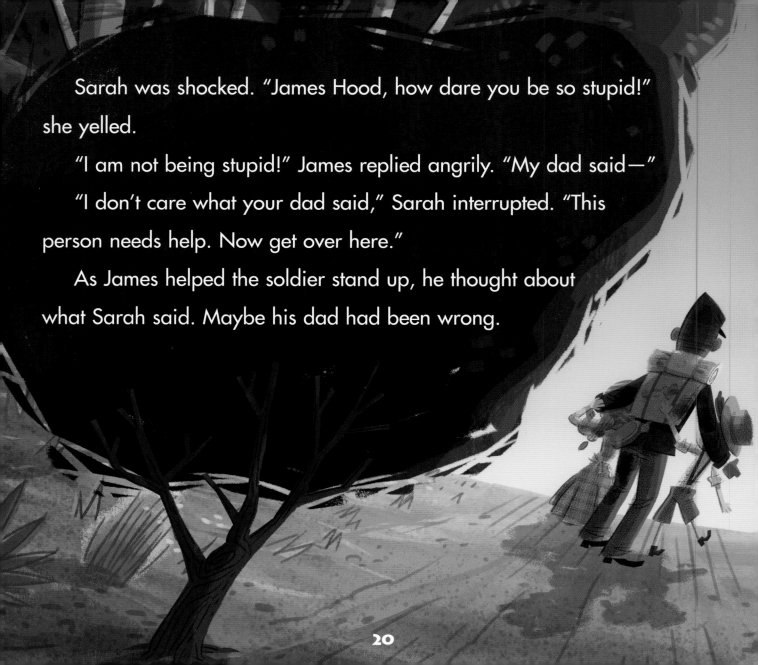

Sarah was shocked. "James Hood, how dare you be so stupid!" she yelled.

"I am not being stupid!" James replied angrily. "My dad said—"

"I don't care what your dad said," Sarah interrupted. "This person needs help. Now get over here."

As James helped the soldier stand up, he thought about what Sarah said. Maybe his dad had been wrong.

STANDING AGAINST SLAVERY

People who worked to end slavery were called **abolitionists**. Many were former slaves and other free black people. Others were white people who recognized how horrible slavery was. Some abolitionists gave speeches and wrote articles. Others helped enslaved people sneak out of the South on the **Underground Railroad**.

Abolitionist Harriet Tubman helped around 70 people escape slavery through the Underground Railroad.

The soldier thanked the two friends as they carefully walked him back to Sarah's house. He told them that his name was Robert. He had been knocked out cold during the battle. When he woke up, his fellow Union soldiers had already moved on.

Sarah's mother began treating Robert's wounds as soon as they arrived. He was badly hurt, but he would survive.

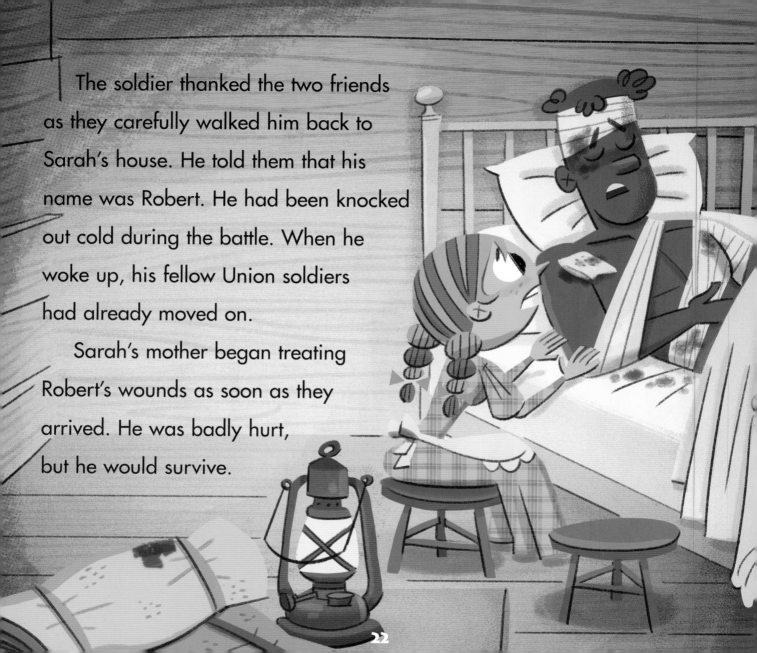

HEALING AT HOME

If you were sick or hurt during the time of the Civil War, it was not always easy to get better. Many of the medications and tools used to heal people today had not been invented. People were much more likely to die from injuries than they are today.

Workers load injured soldiers onto an ambulance after a Civil War battle in 1863.

Robert stayed with Sarah's family for the next few days. Little by little, he began to get better. Each day, James came to visit. Robert had plenty of interesting stories to share. James was amazed as he listened to the soldier describe his daring escape from slavery. As he talked, Sarah and her mother prepared delicious meals for everyone to share.

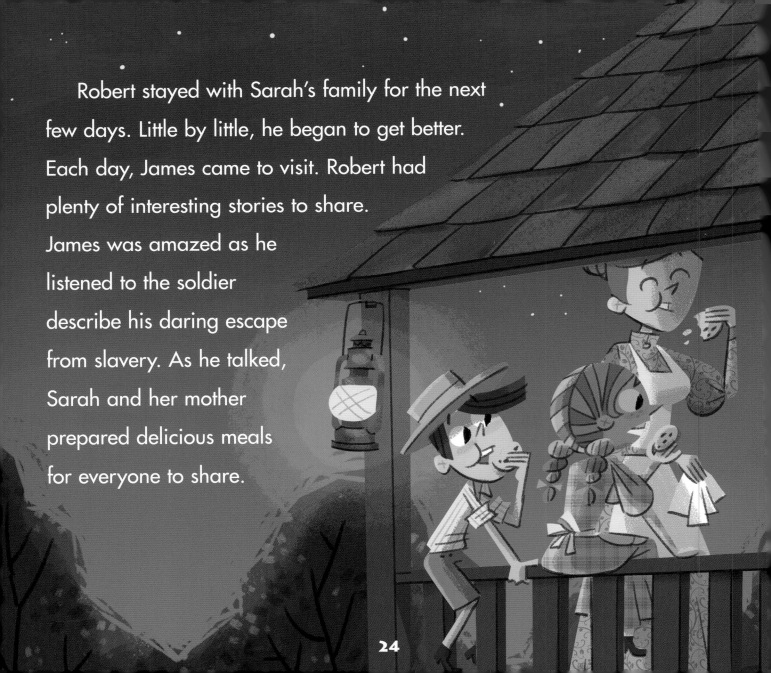

THE COST OF WAR

If you lived during the Civil War, you likely would have known someone who fought for the Union or the Confederacy. Families worried about fathers, sons, and brothers who marched away to battle. Sadly, many never returned home. Experts believe that as many as 750,000 soldiers died of injuries or diseases during the war.

More than 3,500 Union soldiers were buried at Gettysburg National Cemetery in Pennsylvania.

One afternoon a few weeks later, James was waiting for Sarah at their spot. She was late, but she had a surprise that was worth the wait. It was a letter from Robert! In it, he wrote that he was feeling better and living in New York.

James was quiet for a moment after reading the letter. "I'm sure glad we helped him," he said.

"It was the right thing to do," Sarah replied.

James smiled. "Definitely," he agreed.

A TIME OF CHANGE

The Union won the Civil War in 1865. The North and South were once again united. Slavery was made illegal. However, these changes did not solve everything. The South had been heavily damaged by the war. Racism also continued to be a major problem. It still affects our country today.

People had to rebuild homes, farms, railroads, and more after the war.

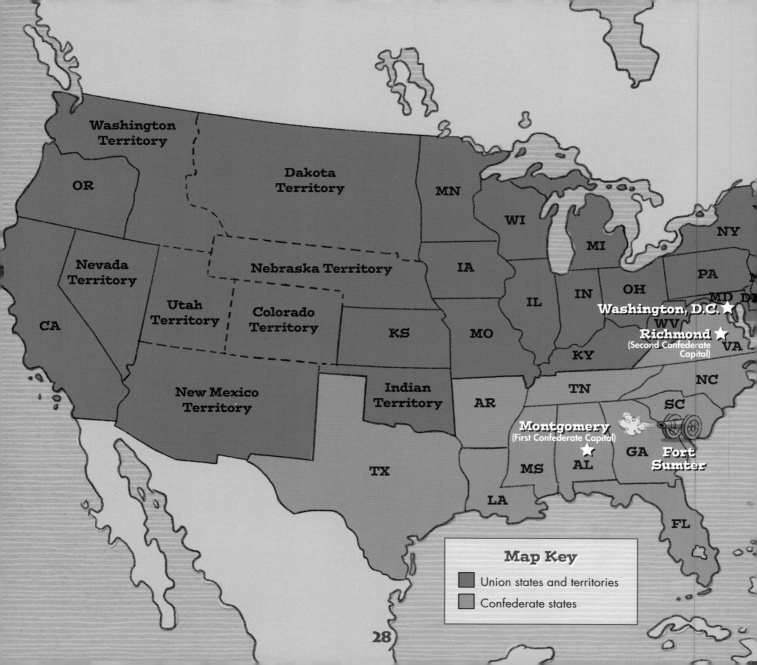

Washington Territory

OR

Nevada Territory

CA

Utah Territory

New Mexico Territory

Dakota Territory

MN

WI

MI

Nebraska Territory

IA

Colorado Territory

KS

MO

Indian Territory

AR

TX

LA

NY

PA

IL

IN

OH

Washington, D.C. ★

MD D

WV

Richmond ★
(Second Confederate Capital)

VA

KY

TN

NC

SC

Montgomery
(First Confederate Capital) ★

MS

AL

GA

Fort Sumter

FL

Map Key
Union states and territories
Confederate states

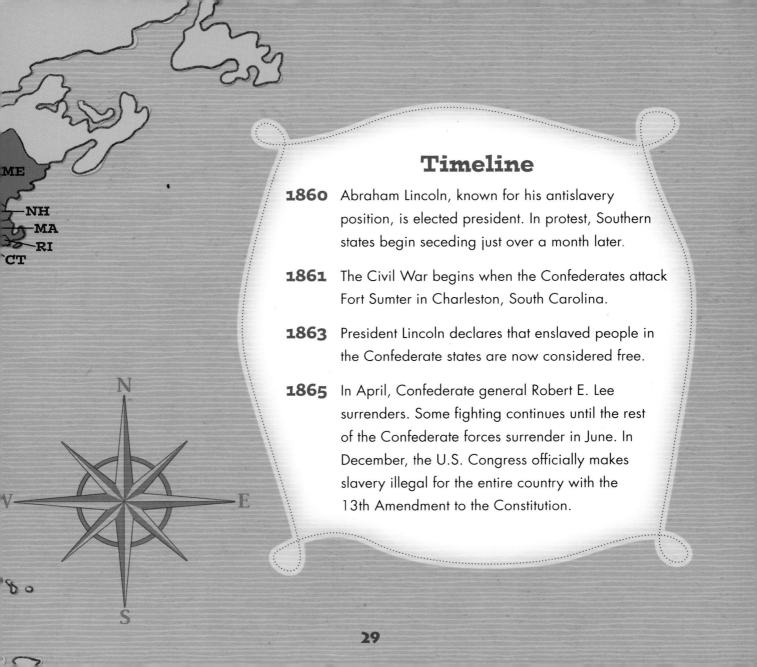

ME

NH
MA
RI
CT

Timeline

1860 Abraham Lincoln, known for his antislavery position, is elected president. In protest, Southern states begin seceding just over a month later.

1861 The Civil War begins when the Confederates attack Fort Sumter in Charleston, South Carolina.

1863 President Lincoln declares that enslaved people in the Confederate states are now considered free.

1865 In April, Confederate general Robert E. Lee surrenders. Some fighting continues until the rest of the Confederate forces surrender in June. In December, the U.S. Congress officially makes slavery illegal for the entire country with the 13th Amendment to the Constitution.

Words to Know

abolitionists (ab-uh-LISH-uh-nists) people who worked to end slavery

enlistment (en-LIST-muhnt) the process of joining the military

racism (RAY-siz-im) unfair or cruel treatment of people based on their race

seceding (si-SEED-ing) officially separating from a group or organization

slavery (SLAY-vuh-ree) the practice of treating people as property that can be bought and sold

Underground Railroad (UHN-dur-ground RAYL-rohd) a system of hiding places in several states that helped enslaved people from the South escape to freedom in the North

Index

ABOUT THE AUTHOR

Wil Mara is a best-selling and award-winning author of more than 150 books, many of which are educational titles for children.

Visit this Scholastic Web site for more information about the Civil War:

www.factsfornow.scholastic.com

Enter the keywords **Civil War**

ABOUT THE ILLUSTRATOR

Roger Zanni is a lot like Bigfoot. He is tall, hairy, friendly, and voracious. However, there are two big differences: he was raised in captivity and he loves drawing for girls and boys of all ages. He regularly creates artwork for kids' magazines, children's books, teen novels, advertisements, and anything else that might be fun and challenging from his sunny hometown of Barcelona, Spain.